Veterans Transition
A Contact Sport

Bernard Bergan

Veterans Transition
A Contact Sport

Bernard Bergan

Veterans Transition-A Contact Sport
Published by: Red Bike Publishing
Copyright © 2017 by Bernard Bergan

Published in the United States of America
www.redbikepublishing.com

Red Bike Publishing also publishes books in electronic format. Some publications appearing in print may not be available in electronic book format.

Library of Congress Control Number: 2017932293
ISBN: 978-1-936800-70-4

CONTENTS

Dedication

To Latashia. Thank you for going to the military recruiter with me, standing with me as I signed up, standing with me as I trained, deployed, redeployed, and transitioned well. You are the unsung Hero of my journey.

"For I know the plans I have for you," declares the LORD, "plans to prosper you and not to harm you, plans to give you hope and a future." Jeremiah 29:11

"The freedom to do your best means nothing unless you are willing to do your best." Colin Powell

"A lot of people resist transition and therefore never allow themselves to enjoy who they are. Embrace the change, no matter what it is; once you do, you can learn about the new world you're in and take advantage of it." Nikki Giovanni

"Don't grow accustomed to living with less, doing less, and being less to the point that you eventually sit back and accept it." Joel Osteen

INTRODUCTION

Since transitioning from the military, I have spoken with hundreds of service members at networking events, mentorship programs, and at Veterans Service Organization events; from these conversations, I knew that there was a need to share more about the principles and strategies that I personally used as I transitioned from the military to a Corporate career.

During many of these conversations, I could see that service members were pleasantly surprised that they already had the tools necessary to transition effectively and maximize the opportunities that would present themselves.

With that I do understand the impact that leaving the military will have on every individual faced with taking that leap. Your personal decision to serve changed the way you looked at the world and as you served you deepened your personal values, your ability to contribute to high performing teams, and most importantly you did your part to secure and defend the freedoms that makes our country The United States of America a beacon of hope in a troubled world.

Transitions can be exciting and terrifying, but as a service member you have some unique advantages when it comes to facing difficult situations and overcoming obstacles. I wrote this book as a reminder of all that you have already overcame, endured, and completed. From basic training to deployments to Countries like Afghanistan you have honorably faced each challenge knowing that you had to bring more than your best to the table every single day then figure out how to improve on your best.

As you prepare to transition take that same work ethic, experience, and grit into your new arena. You can transition to the career and life of your dreams. I hope this book serves as a guide that assists you on your journey from the military to what comes next and provides many of the answers you'll need as you transition.

Chapter 1 Personal Courage

Stepping into the Unknown

I was highly trained for my deployment to Afghanistan. We spent a year and a half preparing with a focus on desert operations. Our mission was clear, we had the right equipment, personnel, and we were prepared to do whatever it takes to accomplish our mission successfully. My unit First Special Forces Group 3rd Battalion had extensive experience navigating this terrain. We were now just going to do it at scale. Everyone felt clear on the mission going in that they knew what they would be asked to do and who they could depend on when things escalated. What still sticks with me is that many of us had never been here before. We were being asked to live in a foreign country and successfully operate on missions that would test our teamwork, our ability to work under pressure, and lastly our personal courage. We stepped into the unknown and accomplished our mission with distinction. Transitioning from the military will require personal courage. Will you make that transition with distinction? I believe you can, but you must lay aside what you think you know and commit to preparing for the journey. This journey can be a lonely one. You are leaving behind women and men who have become as close to you as a family. For me, it meant leaving behind six years' worth of relationships and stepping into the unknown. A commitment to personal courage is a requirement as you relearn what purposeful work will be in this season of your life. It required me letting go of time-tested military tools that worked and carefully choosing new tools that would serve me better as I transitioned. It meant me asking for help and admitting that I was no longer the expert. What I didn't realize at the beginning of my journey was that many Business, Community, and Veteran Leaders were working hard to solve some of the gaps that existed in the military transitions process.

My MSSA Journey

I remember a conversation I had when preparing to exit the Army. One of my commanders called me into his office to listen to my transitions plan. As

I shared with him, he stopped me and said. Bergan, you have been an asset to this unit, and we would love to support your transition, but none of us have transitioned before so we need you to not only transition, but we need you to do it well. That way those of us coming behind you will be able to follow the path you left. That realization challenged me. Before this conversation, I had only looked at transitioning as a process that involved my immediate family. I didn't think of my transition as serving my military family. As I made the rounds to all my required military out briefings, my reservations compounded as I listened to the stories of the soldiers around me. For the first time in six years, I felt the weight of being on a mission without the support of a team. Transitioning well was my goal, but how would I do that. On top of that, I felt this ticking clock to accomplish my transition in the allotted time. I was making my rounds and submitting my resume to the vendors who were on base. My focus was transitioning to the IT industry as it not only peaked my interest, but my research had shown that it had many openings in the Greater Seattle area where I currently lived. As I continued to hand out my resume, one of the individuals called out to me SGT Bergan I turned and approached. After scanning over your resume, I think we have a good fit for your skill set. I listened with a healthy dose of skepticism as they shared their ideas about the Microsoft Software and Systems Academy (MSSA) and what they were trying to accomplish. Their goal was to train soldiers who are still on active duty in their last 16 weeks of military service culminating with a guaranteed interview at Microsoft. As I mulled it over two things were at war within me the guaranteed interview was a major positive, but the fact that this was a pilot program was a major negative. Did I want to be in the test group? What did it mean if I did this and I failed? What would this mean if I spent the last 16 weeks of my transitions time putting all my eggs in the same basket and that basket this program couldn't deliver on its promises? To say I was skeptical is an understatement. I did want to work within the IT industry, but I had never considered working at Microsoft. Lastly, could I commit to 16 weeks of the unknown in a space where no one had done this before?

Two things helped me solidify my decision around being a part of the MSSA pilot program. The first one was in my informational interview with one of the MSSA reps they asked me about my family. It wasn't just a surface level question. We spent the next fifteen minutes discussing how my military transition would affect my family and how transitions programs like this one are designed to fill a gap that many families experience as their service member transitions. The fact that I would still be on active duty as I did my training with the MSSA was a unique benefit of this type of transitions program. The second major indicator that the MSSA was a good fit was when I met many of the women and men who had applied to be in the pilot program. We all had different backgrounds Special Forces Sniper, Marine Engineer Warrant Officer, Cyber Defense NCO; we were all here to try something different and attempt something that seemed impossible. Knowing that I was around people who cared deeply about military families and that I would be around service members who would dare to step into the unknown without looking back reignited my personal courage. I still remember the phone call letting me know that I was one of 21 individuals selected for the pilot program of the MSSA. I remember writing out my vision for the journey and the outcomes that I could control. I remember knowing that I only had sixteen weeks to make this work. I had to stay committed and fully engaged while remaining teachable, coachable, and disciplined. I promised myself that everything I had was what I had to give and the worse that could happen now is that I leave prepared for a career in the IT industry.

As I reflect on where I am today, I can say the hardest part of transitioning was getting started. The personal courage it takes to close the door on one career and step into the unknown can surprise even the most prepared service member. All surprises are not the same, and the surprise of the Microsoft Software and Systems Academy was truly a blessing in disguise.

Notes

Notes

Notes

Chapter 2: First Contact
A Game of Inches

When we are in the military, we sometimes take for granted the constant contact we have with individuals setting us up for success. It starts with Drill Sergeants aligning with you to train and nurture your progress through basic training. It continues as your platoon sergeant systematically measures your physical fitness and duty competencies. All of this combine for a dynamic support system that helps you reach your goals while quickly reminding you when you are off track.

When I decided to transition from the military, I knew I need to create that support system. I knew I needed mentors who could consistently measure when I was moving towards my goal of transitioning to Corporate IT while quickly assisting me when I needed to course correct. These early days of aligning those relationships can be a bit daunting. You have to get creative on aligning your schedule which is already full and sync it with the schedule of a busy professional. What you will find is that those who have journeyed before you the veterans' community are always willing to be helpful if you bring the best of who you are to the table. Being on time, being flexible, and coachable makes this possible. I would say that the impact of finding coaches and mentors who can help you get crystal clear about what the path ahead will require is one of the greatest investments you can make. Making contact can be as simple as looking up the industry that you would like to be in and quickly completing an internet search for veterans in that field. It could also be as formal as joining a Veterans Organization and leveraging those relationships to garner informational interviews with subject matter experts in your chosen field.

What I have found in the hundreds of conversations I have had with transitioning veterans is that there is this deep attachment to who we currently are and the relationships we currently have. One thing we have all learned through our service is to be adaptable. As you adapt from one career to the other keep in mind that this ending is the beginning of something new so embrace it. You will need to tap into your personal courage to make the bold decision of transitioning well.

Letting go of the amazing relationships that you have built throughout your military career can be extremely difficult, but without doing so many transitioning service members do not allow themselves the space to build new relationships and the time these new relationships will need to work.

During my transitions journey, I remember being challenged to make one new contact a week until I was in my new role. While I didn't find this to be difficult, I didn't immediately see the compounded impact of having to execute this assignment. As I committed to the activity of making contact, I saw this new world that previously didn't exist open up to me. Many of those new contacts were passionate about serving the Veterans community and quickly connected me to greater opportunities along my transitions journey.

In our hyper-connected world making contact is not as difficult as it once was, but many still hesitate to reach out and connect with those that can share some wisdom along with anecdotes from their transitions journey. During my personal transitions journey, I made contact around job fairs, tech meetups, and my personal favorite placing a phone call after receiving a business card.

At first, I was very surprised by how open many business professionals were to sharing their expertise. Time and time again I heard the same thing, Serving those who served is a privilege in ways they could never put into words. Many times what was truly shocking is that they thanked me for reaching out.

What are some of the ways that you have attempted

to make contact? Do you have a script that you follow when breaking the ice and allowing others to see that you are willing to be vulnerable and learn something completely new as you take on the challenge of transitioning well? Don't make time an excuse as you persistently and consistently make contact. We are all pressed for time, but I have found that even the busiest professional, when approached with the right level of professionalism and transparency, will stop and have a conversation that can empower your transitions process.

The barriers you face to your success as you transition is a direct result of the quality of the contacts you make along the way. During my military out briefings I made contact with those representing the MSSA and while I wasn't immediately all in I followed up to learn more. In each moment, I led with who I was, why I had reached out, and what I expected to gain from the engagement. This maximized the time we shared and helped me to fully understand the vision of the MSSA and how it could be a part of my transitions journey.

Notes

Notes

CHAPTER 3 THE NEW MISSION
KNOWING YOUR WHY

As you focus on your transitions journey, you might be so overwhelmed by the amount of activity required to transition and all that you are being asked to accomplish that you lose focus on why you choose to transition in the first place. Your why for choosing a new path can be as simple as being at home to see your daughter grow up or as ambitious as starting a Veteran Owned Conglomerate. Whatever you choose, your

Why needs to be clearly defined and deeply impactful. Your Why should challenge you to stay up late and wake up early. Your Why should increase the disciplines that you utilize to make your transitions goals become your new reality.

During my transitions journey, I knew that I had a rare opportunity to pioneer something that had never been attempted before. I knew that if this group of service members could successfully transition to tech that they would be a part of building a bridge for those who would follow. My Why wasn't to simply transition my why was to transition well. I define transitioning well as moving systematically from one opportunity to the next in a way that creates win-wins for all involved.

My why allowed me to stay focused despite the many opportunities for distraction. My personal Why allowed me to tap into what I had learned during all my years of military training. I remember spending 18 hours each weekend for 16 weeks working on what was required. Military service has taught you to be vigilant, to exist outside of comfort zones, and to thrive in ambiguous high-pressure states. Transitioning well can feel like that sometimes. I know it seems difficult applying the same mindset to your new mission of transitioning, but your why will bring what is required of you during this process into focus. Your commitment to always placing the mission first is what I want to bring to your mind. Do you want to simply transition or Do you want to transition well? The New Mission is to define your Why. Once you have your why then commit to doing whatever it takes to learn the skills to accomplish the mission.

At times, your transitions journey could feel like trying to take a drink of water from a fire hose. There will be so much useful information to sort through and at times it will seem like everyone will have a pitch about who you can become if you follow what they are asking of you. At these moments you need to get clear and silence the noise so you can focus in on your why.

My challenge for you is to find out what does transitioning well look like for you? Follow that answer up with who exactly is depending on you to be a hero as you transition? Write their names down. Write down what it would mean to be able to deliver a new way of life as you transition. Now let's tap into who is depending on you to lead in your community? Think of one organization that you could add value to by bringing your values based military leadership to the table. Write it down. What will transitioning well mean for your brothers and sisters in arms, service members who will be looking to you for guidance and mentorship as they prepare for their transitions journey? Write at least ten names down. Taking the time to answer these questions will help you deepen your why. This list of family, friends, community organizations, and your military family will keep you aligned with whatever it will cost you to be your best as you transition.

My list consisted of my wife, my nephews, and nieces, my mom, and dad, the extended family at my church, and the kids at the local rec center that I volunteered at before enlisting. I also added those in my unit who I knew would be transitioning shortly after me. In the tough times of learning to code. I took out my list. I read the names carefully thinking of the impact that my success would mean for each group, organization, or person. I didn't forget that I was also transitioning for myself. I had served honorably for six years, and I was excited to see what would come next.

Notes

Notes

Chapter 4: Zeroing in on the Target

Be a Sniper

As you are preparing to leave the military, you are bombarded with the excitement of all the possibilities that are before you. Like me many of you are going to ask yourself should I go back to school? Should I start a new career or am I leaving the military a bit prematurely? In your excitement over the plethora of choices that you have, you might miss the chance to ask yourself some of the most critical questions that you must have answers to at this moment. Questions like Why am I transitioning? What do I expect to have at the end of my transitions process? Lastly, What does transitioning well look like for my family and What does transitioning well mean to me?

Once those questions are answered it is time to zero in on the target. Zeroing in on the target could mean many different things. For me, it meant locking in on a career in the IT industry by learning all I could about what it meant to work at that level. I allowed myself to go into a deployed state where the mission was what woke me up in the morning and the last thing I had in my sights before I went to bed at night.

As a transitioning service member, you might feel that a shotgun approach to transitioning might serve you better. You might want to spread your focus around firing at multiple opportunities hoping that something anything is the right thing. Remember this no one goes to a special school to learn to use a shotgun, but snipers are always treated with deep respect. You will have to become a sniper with the target that you choose. You will have to lock sites on it. Perform all due diligence on what could hinder you from hitting your target with the one shot you have. One by one you will then have to eliminate these hindrances to gain the right vantage point. As you take aim, you will have to quiet all the doubts, all the fears, and then you will have to execute.

Pulling the trigger of transitions is a wake-up call for everyone who has accomplished it. The time freedom that you hoped to realize is balanced by the deep need to reconnect with loved ones. The systematic day to day existence of military service is replaced by the noise of choices from what to wear to who you get to spend time with. The freedom you have to travel is in contrast with the direct need to feel grounded and on purpose. As you zero in on your target, you will have to face these questions every day. You will want to question the mission, you will want increased clarity on your orders, but I know from experience as a soldier, as a husband, and as a community leader during transitions, you do not have the luxury of indecision. Making the decision to pull the trigger and execute the daily habits that will take you to your goals is the only way ahead.

What has been stopping you from zeroing in? If you have found your why for transitioning and you have put the shotgun approach to transitioning away what self-talk should you adapt to make sure you are executing the new mission?

Anyone who has been through the Microsoft Software and Systems Academy can tell you that it is a coding boot camp on steroids. The challenge is not for the faint of heart, but neither is being trained to deploy anywhere in the world to defend your country. The MSSA required execution every single day for sixteen weeks, but the target was clear. Not only would I have an opportunity to interview at a company that had proven itself in the marketplace, but I would also receive training while on active duty that would empower me for the rest of my life.

As you zero in on what's just over the horizon lock sights on what is up next in your journey by knowing your why. Get clear about your new mission and know that you have what it takes to execute that mission. You will need to tap into personal courage as you make contact and ask for help. Just know that you are not in this alone. There are many women and men working hard to assist you in your decision to transition. The temptation to use a shotgun approach to transitioning will be there, but I challenge you to be disciplined in your training and take focused steps towards what is next.

Notes

Notes

Chapter 5: The Step Before the Step

Knowing How to Train

Now that you clearly have your target in your sights. Knowing how to train is what you should focus on. I know you are chomping at the bit to start training, but without knowing how to train you can invest a lot of time and energy getting prepared in the wrong way. When I attended Airborne School at Ft. Benning in Georgia I found many of the routine drills to be extremely difficult. Even basic exercises like the flutter kick or pull ups were proving extremely difficult. After an extremely long day of training, a fellow soldier said to me Bergan it's your boots. See I was wearing my winter boots almost the entire time I was training. It was winter so of course right place right time right uniform. The extra weight wasn't helpful in helping me to train effectively and once I course corrected training went a whole lot better.

How are you approaching your training for what's next? Are you finding best practices from industry leaders and mentors? I know the easy thing to do would be to show up right place right time right uniform and hope it works out, but there is always room for improvement, and you can always find a better way.

I found that asking others exactly what they did yielded high impact results in my transitions journey. As you move beyond your career in the military variety in training will increase. Many times people want to share with you what they think you should do, but knowing what they did is way more helpful.

We all learn differently, but in the military, we all trained the same. Now that you have a chance to train the way you learn best you might still struggle with your default to being trained the same even if it is ineffective.

During my transitions, journey learning how I learned was of absolute importance. I didn't want to spend time training ineffectively because I did not look for different approaches that resonated more deeply with me than others. I had world class instructors as I learned a new skill. I was challenged by the workload, and at times I found the material to be overwhelming.

What I found was that when tested I was able to perform well even though I didn't feel that I had mastered the material. I dug deep to deconstruct my approach to how I prepare for tests. I found that I consistently had taken smaller tests that gave me immediate feedback. That immediate feedback was one of the ways I learned best.

In the military, the constant feedback or on the spot correction does not allow you to lose your way completely. There is always someone who is helping you to course correct. As you take on the new challenge of knowing how to train you might find yourself needing mentors and allies who can help you with that course correction.

Do you know how you learn best? Have you challenged your default setting of wanting to train for your new opportunity like everyone else? What advantages would you have if you mastered how you learn?

Knowing how to train was one of the keys to unlocking what was next for me. I had spent six years in the military training with the most elite athletes on the planet. These soldiers trained to go into any environment anywhere in the world and perform with precision while keeping perspective and overcoming any unforeseen changes to the plan. I knew that if I brought these qualities to my new mission, I would also be able to master what was in front of me.

Your journey is yours, but I challenge you to unlock the tools you already have. Knowing how you learn and what you already have within you will allow you to make the shifts necessary to lock in on your goal. As challenges arise in unforeseen ways your ability to adapt and overcome will be a necessary tool that will keep you marching towards your target. The accountability that mentorship brings during this process will help you refine how you learn. As you get better at mastering what is in front of you, those small wins will lead to bigger wins and as the wins continue you would have transitioned well.

Notes

Notes

Chapter 6: Mentorship 101

Knowing Your Allies

Knowing who has your back is one of the keys to successful military service. It is also one of the keys to a successful military transition. Having allies in this fight for a new career will prove meaningful along your journey. Do not go this alone. There are many parts of transitioning that you must face alone. The decision to transition is yours alone. Your Why is also yours alone.

What you will transition to is also a singular decision, but there is no excuse for not including mentors for everything else.

In the Military, we all have mentors we don't call them mentors we usually call them platoon sergeants, drill sergeants, or commanders. These are people who know what our goals are from small to large then they hold us accountable for the daily, weekly, and monthly activity that take us towards our final destination. Do you have mentors as you prepare to transition? Who are some of the allies you can reach out to that will hold you accountable? Create a list of ten people and reach out to them. Attach a copy of your vision for your transitions and allow them the access to hold you accountable.

One of the strangest military concepts for me was that of having a battle buddy. A battle buddy was someone who you were accountable to at all times. If they failed you failed and if they succeeded you succeeded as well. I didn't get why having a battle buddy was so relevant until I started to see what could occur when you avoided the disciplines of being accountable to someone else. Having someone to push you, keep you focused, and dialed in enhances your ability to rise to the occasion. As you are transitioning in addition to great mentors, identify someone who can be your battle buddy during this journey. Someone who will challenge you to succeed despite what obstacles you are facing. Someone who sees exactly what the journey requires, but is unwilling to let you doubt that you can overcome those obstacles by breaking them down into bite-sized tasks that you can master each day. My battle buddies reminded me even at 3 am some Saturday mornings that this journey I was on and the guaranteed interview I was being offered was nothing less than remarkable, and I would have to deliver a remarkable effort to deliver on it.

I was fully committed to transitioning well, and doing the work. I had great battle buddies in place and allowed them to hold me accountable every step of the way. What I found was that there were still some gaps in what I needed to understand in leaving the military and becoming successful within a corporate environment. That is where my mentors came in. They brought their experience, their expertise and helped me fill the gaps in my experience and perspective. As I previously mentioned, one of my mentors challenged me to meet someone new every week until I started my new role. Another one of my mentors challenged me to get my resume completed and to share my resume with two employers every week until I had completed my transitions. My mentors taught me the importance of informational interviews. I learned not just how to make first contact with individuals, but how to sustain those relationships by bringing deep value to each interaction. Here are some questions for you. What gaps have you identified in your transitions process? Who can you contact that will help you fill those gaps? How will you partner with a mentor as you continue your transitions process? What other allies can you invite to the table as you continue this journey?

Notes

Chapter 7: Trust the Process

The Road Ahead

The road ahead for many transitioning veterans can be a lonely one. Even with the right mentors and allies the hours and hours of study, self-development, and stepping outside of your comfort zone will challenge all that you know and all that you are. The process can be overwhelming. This process will include training, interviewing, resume building, and building your personal network. Your mentors will open new doors for you, but it is up to you to walk through them. When things get difficult, and it will you have to dig your heels in and trust the process.

In my second week of basic training, our Drill Sergeants treated our platoon to a special PT session in which their goal was to make the walls sweat. Upon completion, we were left to ponder this idea if you trust what this is designed to do you will become a better soldier. If you resist and remain inflexible, you will break.

Transitioning well does not have to break you. Its only purpose is to aid you in redesigning your life from what it is to what it could become.

What could your life look like if you completed your resume? What would it look like if you completed that job application? What would your life look like if you completed that transitions program? How about your college degree?

Transitioning from the Military can be sudden or gradual. One thing remains constant. You have to own it. You can complete the journey by breaking it down into manageable parts and executing immediately on what you learn.

The road ahead won't always be clear. When things lack clarity, do not use that as a reason to hesitate. That is when you need to lean in visualize the road ahead trusting the process. My military transitions journey was full of moments where trusting the process was the only choice. No one had ever attempted what we were pioneering as MSSA students. The course work was extremely demanding, and there were no easy victories. Every question only led to more questions. These unanswered questions would at times pile up threatening to immobilize and unravel all the progress that we had made. I had to tap into many of the lessons I had learned as a soldier and commit to seeing it through to the very end. One of my strategies was visualizing which was more difficult. I had survived basic training, airborne school, and had deployed to some of the toughest regions of the world with that in mind how could I let a class get the best of me.

As a transitioning service member, you might be tempted to innovate in your approach to overcoming adversity. What I know from my transitions journey is that the same mental, physical, and strategic approaches to overcoming adversity that you mastered through the rigors of military training can, if adapted to your current challenges, bring you success in these new environments as well. Your military service is proof that you can endure long hours, your service is proof that you can rise to the occasion digging deep down to accomplish the mission. The same personal courage and grit will serve you as you transition. You will have to find strategic approaches to willing yourself to win, and each win will compound to get you closer to your transitions goals.

When things seem difficult as you face the road ahead your commitment to trusting the process will empower your will to win.

Notes

CHAPTER 8: REPOSITION YOURSELF
WINNING SMALL TO WIN BIG

For many of us, the idea of repositioning ourselves seems at odds with everything we were trained to do. Military precision requires solving problems at scale while remaining committed to the team. Orders are what allowed you to reposition, and without permission, moving on was not an option. Don't anticipate the command still, echoes in my subconscious as I strategize and plan what is next for my family and I. This truth served me well when working in a mass formation in which we all had to move as one. As I transitioned, however, anticipating what was next and preparing for the new mission was what allowed me to turn small wins into big wins.

During my last two years in the military, I moved my family from twenty minutes outside the base to over an hour away. I had relocated my family to Downtown Seattle so that we could start to observe what life could be like once we had completed our military transitions. There was a lot of relevant feedback on this move. My Platoon Sergeant was concerned that I wouldn't be able to make it in on time if we had rapid deployment needs. My fellow soldiers and peers voiced concerns that my family wouldn't be as safe as when we lived in a traditional military community. All of these concerns were relevant, and I allowed myself to learn from this feedback while focusing on my need to reposition myself.

What I didn't know when we first moved was that many of my mentors lived in Seattle. The small wins from moving to Seattle stacked up becoming big wins as my network within the tech community continued to expand. Though the decision was not popular with my chain of command at the time, it proved to be the right decision for my family and me despite the pushback. Turning small wins into big wins should be a focus of your strategy as you transition. You might not have the time to make sure every decision that you make is right, but you can build on each decision until it reveals its deeper strategic value.

If you look closely, you will discover deep value in every step of your military journey. The same strategies that allowed you to win in one arena will allow you to excel as you transition. Each military school that I attended required a shift to a different location. That repositioning allowed me to minimize distractions while focusing on what I was sent there to accomplish. Whether it was airborne school or advanced training in my military specialty without being repositioned the sacrifices needed to focus on my immediate goals would have been muted by the noise of daily routines.

The military infused in all the service members the power of daily habits and routines. These small wins' lead to bigger wins that combine to produce the desired effect. In your transitions process, your daily habits will have to change. Habits like waking up early to make your morning formations might become waking up early to study for an IT certification. The habit of spending two hours at the gym might be adjusted to spend one hour at the gym and the next hour at a career center training for your new role. As you look through your daily routines, ask yourself what can I tweak or adjust to reposition myself. As you make, these adjustments small wins will become big wins. These adjustments might not require you to move over an hour away, but they will highlight how you can reposition yourself.

Notes

Chapter 9: Learning from the Journey of Others

Self Assessment

One of the amazing things that my mentors did for me as I transitioned was to talk about the lessons they learned during their transition. Some of my Mentors went straight to work after completing their military careers while others journeyed back to school, and some did both. They talked about going all in adjusting to a different pace of life while course correcting when necessary. The ability to make corrections along the

way to self-assess is something we all benefited from
in the military. On a high performing team, you might
not have the time to answer all your questions and ad-
dress all your doubts. You must act. While you are taking action, you self-assess categorizing your strengths
and what you bring to the table. You also look at your
weaknesses deciding if they will be harmful to the
mission or are they something you can manage as you
zero in on your goals. Make a decision then make that
decision right. Learning from the transition stories
of others helped me to see beyond the immediate
obstacles. I saw that as they transitioned they made a
decision then, they put everything on the table to make
that decision the right decision.

This knowledge empowered me during my MSSA
journey. I had made a decision. Now I had to do the
work to make this decision right. Many transitioning
service members forget that they are empowered to
endure to the very end. Transitioning well might mean
getting so focused that you choose to stop watching
television. It might mean twelve-hour study sessions on
Saturdays. It might mean waking up at two-thirty every
day, so you have an hour to study before reporting for
duty. Are you committed to self-assessing and finding
the gaps in your preparation? Self-assessment, every
step of the way, allowed me to fill in one of the critical
gaps in my transitions approach.

I knew that there was an aspect of competition to
secure my a role with Microsoft. My self-assessment
showed me that if we all trained the same and we all
had access to the same tools, uniformity would once
again make finding the right candidate a needle in a

haystack for Microsoft. During my self-assessment, one question that kept reoccurring was How was I going to present my best self each time and gain some advantages along the way?

One thing that many overlook when choosing to pursue a specific career is a cultural fit. I knew that I would have to dive deep into tech culture learning what it would be like to work at a software company. To that end, I did as many informational interviews as my schedule permitted. I met women and men at Microsoft's who showcased the company culture and embodied the company values. I was excited to see the similarities, and I was challenged to overcome some of the differences. As I worked to adapt to tech culture, it deepened my resolve that Microsoft was the right fit for me and the MSSA was the conduit to get there.

During my guaranteed interview what resonated deeply with many of my interviewers was that I showcased not only the company values but the company culture. My research, self-study, and determination showcased that not only was I able to do the work but I would work to excel at each task. At the end of 2013, Microsoft was a company in transition and with that came amazing new opportunities to be a part of a culture that was shifting to a growth mindset. This theme of having a growth mindset was a major discovery as I prepared. The military has many storied traditions, but we produce the best of the best through good strategies, consistent input from others, and hard work. I had spent six years practicing what Microsoft was transitioning to, and I knew from first-hand experience that I would be an asset to that culture.

Notes

Chapter 10: Mindset 101
Your Soldiers Creed

I am an American Soldier.
I am a warrior and a member of a team.
I serve the people of the United States, and live the Army Values.
I will always place the mission first.
I will never accept defeat.
I will never quit.
I will never leave a fallen comrade.
I am disciplined, physically and mentally tough, trained and proficient in my warrior tasks and drills.
I always maintain my arms, my equipment and myself.
I am an expert, and I am a professional.
I stand ready to deploy, engage, and destroy, the enemies of the United States of America in close combat.
I am a guardian of freedom and the American way of life.
I am an American Soldier.

Every day, during my first six months in the army I had to recite the Soldiers Creed. It ensured that I knew what I had chosen to become. It ensured I knew what it meant to be an AMERICAN SOLDIER. For the next six years, Life tested me on the merits of this creed not just to see if I had these words committed to memory, but to make sure I understood how I was expected to perform when everything was on the line.

As you prepare to transition, you will need to find a creed. Find something that challenges you to maintain the highest levels of discipline while remaining physically and mentally tough. If you have already transitioned, you know the importance of bringing professionalism to what you do daily. Your creed should empower you to unleash values based leadership on the communities you impact the most. It should highlight who you are, who you serve, and who you are becoming. Most importantly your creed shapes your mindset.

As a Military service member, your mindset was clear. You lived as a warrior and a member of a Team. You knew that you were expected to guard the freedoms of all Americans and maintain your tactical expertise. You knew that you stood ready if called to deploy, engage, and face our countries enemies. You knew to quit and be defeated were not choices that you had. Lastly, you knew that values based leadership was what you would bring to the table each and every day. When you recited, this creed surprises were rare. You stayed ready.

What empowers you to stay ready now? Are you mentally checked out? Overwhelmed even. My challenge to you is that you take a few moments and tailor the soldiers creed to you. Think of the roles that you will excel at as you transition well. Start with your values and build to your family. Look at the industry that you are working towards. How are you going to become proficient in the tasks of your new career? Are you committed to maintaining your skills and applying a growth mindset to everything that you do? I challenge you to become an expert at what you have chosen to pursue. Can you become that expert? Absolutely.

Holding myself accountable by having a creed to which I subscribed embedded in me an obsession with improving and getting better. Just like the Soldiers Creed brought energy to every situation in which it was recited your personal creed should push and elevate you to rise to the occasion every single day. I know living by your personal creed every day with no days off can bring with it some anxiety, but without having a personal creed, it's easy to lose sight of who you must become to accomplish your new mission. I want you to continue holding yourself to the highest values and standards just like you did when you served. Could you have endured your longest days in the military pushing yourself to take that extra step and inch by inch overcoming the challenges that we all faced without knowing in detail that you were overcoming because you were a guardian of our freedoms and the American way of Life? Your personal creed is designed to do the same thing. In your longest days of committing to transitioning well and in facing your limitations. You will be able to tap into your personal creed and remember that there are those who look to you as an example of

Professionalism, Leadership, and Expertise.

Notes

Notes

Chapter 11: You Don't Know What You Don't Know

Remain Open To Change

As you forge ahead on your journey to transitioning well, change can be a welcomed ally. There is no harm in admitting that you don't know what you don't know. Your commitment to military service and the sacrifices required kept you locked into a greater purpose with a specific strategy. As you transition, your daily strategy will need the flexibility to adapt to what you are learning each step of the way. You also do not know if that strategy is designed to produce the results you desire. The ability to adapt and overcome the pressures inherent with transitioning well will allow you the flexibility to bend in this season if necessary but never break as you rise to the occasion.

During my military transitions, I had many moments where I quickly had to self-assess and admit what I didn't know. I did not know how to create a modern resume. I also did not know how to demystify what I did in the military and apply it to the civilian sector. As I admitted these truths to myself, I remained open to change. I didn't waste time learning to do something that I didn't need to learn how to do. I partnered with experts whether mentors, business leaders and career coaches in completing my resume. Together the resume that we produced was a far superior to what I had attempted to produce on my own.

What is hindering your process as you transition? Is it something that you must master to succeed? If it requires mastery, commit to finding an approach that will empower you to master it. If mastery is not required, find the experts and partner with them. By remaining open to change, you enhance your awareness of how best to approach each leg of your journey.

My MSSA journey was full of opportunities to admit that I didn't know what I didn't know. Not only was I learning software development at the highest level there were also required coding projects along the way. Many of those projects needed to be completed not mastered. My first approach was mastery wanting to know within the week I was given for a project every detail of the assignment. I wanted to know how to reproduce the results on my own and a history of why this is important.

What gave me perspective was remembering military boot camp. During our Morning runs, we all ran 5 miles or more daily. Depending on your PT scores you were assigned to a specific run group. The goal was not to make you a world class runner it was to build your endurance by consistently having you commit to long runs at a pace that challenged you. If my focus was on mastering running; I wouldn't have stayed committed to the daily goal which was completing each run.

The same held true for my projects. The goal was exposure to different concepts of programming and programming languages. Working each project to completion helped me to get a top-down view of all the choices you have as a programmer. Before taking the course, I had only researched the programming languages that Microsoft had specialized in or designed. Each coding project forced me to see what I didn't know, and this allowed me to become more aware of which experts I would have to tap into to as I needed to partner along the way.

Are you open to change as you transition? Have you identified the areas that require mastery and the areas that require you to shut up, show up, and complete the run? Getting out of your own way might prove difficult but as you commit to identifying what should be mastered and what should simply be completed you will have more time to access the experts and learn the secrets of their expertise.

Notes

Chapter 12: Constructive Criticism

Secret to Accessing Experts

Most of the feedback on your transitions journey will come from people who mean well, but who have never walked a day in your boots. The easy way out would be to ignore all of the free expert advice and forge ahead without asking yourself what part of what was shared specifically applied to me. Being able to self-assess daily is one of the tools that you will need when you transition, but combining self-assessment with constructive criticism will empower you with a framework that enhances your ability to take consistent action on your behalf accelerating the progress you will make to transitioning well.

One of my mentors challenged me on day one of my transitions journey to produce a shareable resume by the end of that week. I researched current resume formats; I downloaded all relevant templates, and I produced what I felt was a shareable resume. When I shared my resume with my mentor the feedback was immediate Bernard none of this applies to civilian careers. I had done my best but not having to produce a resume for the past six years was not to my benefit. With my mentors help and working with industry experts I was able to apply that constructive criticism to produce a shareable resume within a few days. When I thought I was completed, I was challenged to submit my resume to businesses that peaked my interest every week. I didn't understand why any of this was important, but through that activity, I received a callback. Bernard, I have your resume in front of me, and you have a lot of solid experience are you online do you have a social profile a LinkedIn perhaps? Again I did my research and saw the value that a business network like LinkedIn could have on my transition. I created a profile after researching all the best ideas for showcasing your work history online. When I shared my LinkedIn profile with my mentor the steps I had taken the feedback again was immediate. Bernard here is how LinkedIn is used within your industry, but what would be most helpful for what you are working on is having a GitHub.

As you can clearly imagine the feedback was endless what I choose to focus on was the intention of that feedback. I humbly allowed each moment of constructive criticism to fuel my journey by making me aware of some of the gaps in my transitions process. As I filled the gaps what I found was that experts in various fields started to notice. Not only did they notice, but they reached out to assist me along the way. Unlike mentors, experts are not interested in the daily, weekly, or monthly activity of your transitions journey. Their goal is to sharpen your impact. They share their knowledge with those who have made it through the early stages and have risen to a level that can only be improved by what an expert brings to the table.

What would having access to industry experts mean to your transitions journey? For me, those experts made sure I was aware of the tools utilized by working professionals at Microsoft to build the software and services that the company produced. While the MSSA prepared me to do the work; experts showcased for me a day in the life. Seeing first hand what the hard work was going to produce enhanced my commitment to do the work.

Receiving feedback from experts reminded me of on the spot corrections we all received while serving in the military. This feedback is not to be taken personally. You received it because there is an area in which you can improve and if you immediately course correct, you embody who you will become once you master each skill.

What is standing between you and the expert advice that you would need to transition well? Is it your inability to self-assess? What is your approach to accepting constructive criticism? Are you committed to improving your approach to what you do with the feedback you receive? Have you identified the experts that have shown up to advise you? Receiving this feedback and making the adjustments will empower you on your journey of transitioning well. I challenged you to apply what you learn from constructive criticism it will enhance your ability to train pushing you to exceed the standards of your new industry.

Notes

Notes

Chapter 13: Train to Standard
Don't Watch the Clock

Nothing drains the energy of a soldier more than the concept of time. We all endured basic training. We had to endure the discipline of being on guard twenty-four hours or more. Many of us have been deployed and stationed all over the globe which required us to adapt to eighteen-hour work days and seven-day work weeks. We have all pushed past the basic need to stay on a schedule and reaped the rewards of those few who train beyond our time limits remembering that exceeding the standard is what ends a training session. This concept if mastered will accelerate your small wins as you prepare to transition well.

Day one of being assigned to my unit First Special Forces Group 3rd Battalion I was told in no uncertain terms the PT standards here is 270 if you fall below that we kick you out of the unit. I served in this unit my entire military career. Exceeding the standard should always enhance your goals. We all know that we must take advantage of the opportunity within the timeline of the opportunity, but if you are unable to fully perform a task competently in which you can confidently exceed the standard will it matter in the long run that you finished within the allotted time.

My first time shooting during the Army Weapons Qualification Course I hit twenty-seven targets in a row. Bergan, I heard the drill, Sergeant bellow. Who taught you how to shoot? Drill Sergeant I said. I did some shooting in boy scouts. My drill sergeant looked at me and said have you ever fired an M-16 before today. I answered No drill sergeant. He said to me your done go clean your weapon. For the next eight hours, I cleaned my weapon. What I didn't know was that my twenty-seven was just enough to qualify I could have gotten better, but good enough was all I achieved that day. In the military, we train to the standard, not to time. That simply means the only reason to end training is when every member of your team can exceed the standard. What stayed with me all these years later was the soldier who had never fired a weapon before a day in her life. Instead of spending eight hours cleaning her weapon she spent eight hours learning to fire her weapon learning to exceed the standard. She left the range shooting forty out of forty.

What is your forty out of forty? As you transition, you will feel the pressures of time running out. You will feel overwhelmed with thoughts that compound that pressure leaving you more aware of time than ever before. You might even say to yourself there is not enough time to truly understand all of what I'm being asked to learn. What is powerful is that Military Service members have all exceeded this pressure before. Yes, your concerns are valid but don't allow concerns to become excuses. Training is designed to teach you something. Find out what that is and then do everything in your power to learn it regardless of the time constraints you feel you have. Don't focus on being perfect. Hitting twenty-seven in a row without missing is a great start, but if you spend the next eight hours cleaning your weapon, it's a horrible finish. Training to standard simply means training beyond the self-limiting boundaries we adhere to when we set our mind to accomplish something. Knowing the benchmarks of your new industry is critical and will allow you to train towards the highest target in your new industry.

During your time in the military, All the training that you received was very systematic. There were no question and answer sessions. The way that your instructors knew you needed additional help was by pushing you to the point of failure and exposing your limitations. Once these limitations were exposed, you then were scheduled for retraining. I have learned never to watch the clock as I train. By bending time to the standard, I can push past the boundaries inherent in any task. I can see in my approach if there are additional disciplines that I should expose myself to as I work to understand what I'm learning. I then self-assess to see if I am distracted by the illusion of perfection and missing the lessons inherent in mastery. I used these simple truths to steady the way ahead as I did everything in my power to exceed the standard in my transition from the military.

Notes

Notes

CHAPTER 14: RESET YOUR VISION

RESUPPLYING THE VISION

During my time in Afghanistan right around the
ninth month of consistently executing the mission,
recovering from setbacks, and preparing to forge ahead
despite all we had endured something occurred that
made a deep impression on me. We had visitors who
came in to boost our morale and remind us that what
we were doing mattered in ways we would never fully
understand. That visit allowed us to reset our vision
and sharpened our resolve to see the mission through

to the end. Having someone come in to resupply the vision was the catalyst we needed to make it successfully through the end of our tour.

There will always be moments when the stresses of transition cause your vision to blur. The self-doubt can creep up, and the rejections you face along the way can crush your hopes of finding the balance that you desire. It is in those moments that you will have to allow others to resupply the vision. During my MSSA journey, my vision of transitioning well met with challenges at every level. During many of my longest days, I saw my vision start to blur. Fortunately for me, my vision was resupplied every step of the way.

For someone to resupply the vision they would need to know what the vision is and where you are along the journey. When was the last time you read your vision for your transition? When was the last time that you shared your vision with someone who is on a similar journey or in a position to resupply the vision?

Do not forget this far into your journey that you are on a team. Each member of your team has a specific role to play. You are on the frontlines of transitioning well. You are going to have to interview for new roles. You are going to have to network meet new people and step beyond your comfort zone. You are going to have to fill out that career application. You will have to meet with that college advisor. Your team will need an after action report. Your team will need access to the steps you are taking to track your progress. Your team will need to hear you rehearse the new mission. Your team will need to see your resolve as you trust the process and finish what you have started.

During my transitions journey, I wanted the hard numbers. I wanted to know how many veterans failed each year at transitioning well. I wanted to know what approach these veterans had taken to transitioning and what I could learn from that data. It was a tough set of conversations to have, but one of the patterns I uncovered was that they choose to transition in isolation. These veterans had a plan, they executed on that plan, but somewhere along their journey, they failed to course correct. These veterans had made a decision and had committed to making that decision right, but a lack of mentorship, battle buddies, and community thwarted their efforts.

Transitioning well will test your personal courage. It will provide unique challenges that will require creativity, sacrifice, and discipline to overcome. Your vision will be tested, but you can do this. You can transition well. Find your allies and allow them to hold you accountable. For those seeking a new career find mentors in that career field and learn the answers to some of the questions that you currently have. For those going back to school make contact with the Military and Veterans Support Office at your college or university bring your unique perspective to the table and learn from the journey of others.

As you transition the desire to go it alone will threaten the idea that you are part of a team. When that starts to occur, look around for the teams that you are on and do your part to resupply their vision. That will require you to serve selflessly.

Notes

Chapter 15: Selfless Service

Building Community by Giving Back

I believe that Veterans are the Key to Unlocking America's Next Golden Age. By empowering and influencing one million veterans to transition well and become leaders in their communities we can unlock our country's destiny and continue to change the world. The global impact of my military service is something that will stay with me throughout my entire life. Even on my longest days in the military days that at times lasted 72 hours, there was a deep sense of purpose and belonging. My military leaders were tough, but fair shouldering the intense responsibility of training troops for the reality of being on the front lines. I am thankful for the values-based leadership that permeates daily life within the military. The accountability and camaraderie made the pressures of service bearable because I knew I was not serving in isolation.

You are not transitioning in isolation. There is an entire Nation that is thankful that you suited, up showed up, and stayed ready. Your personal courage, vigilance, and commitment to the mission impacted the world. When you consider what you plan to do next and what it will take to make that become a reality, I challenge you to continue the global impact that you have already had.

When service members ask me Bernard why Microsoft. You are skilled, you have an incredible work ethic, and you would be a great fit for any company. I always share two stories. The first is my journey through the MSSA and my skepticism that Microsoft would deliver on its promises. Microsoft wanted to deliver this Academy at scale by building partnerships nationwide, and to date, we have accomplished that. To the women and men who made my MSSA journey possible from ideation to implementation, I want to say thank you.

My second story is of Microsoft's global giving program. In my second year with the company, Microsoft employees raised a record-breaking $125 million for more than 18,000 nonprofits and schools across the globe. This was the greatest year-over-year increase ever - and the fifth year in a row that they raised more than $100 million (information as provided at *https://www.microsoft.com/en-us/philanthropies/our-employees/employee-giving/*). That Global Impact in Philanthropy resonates deeply with me. Microsoft matches employee nonprofit donations and volunteering year-round. The global impact of philanthropy as a benefit keeps me passionate about our companies mission of empowering every person and every organization on the planet to achieve more.

Now that you are prepared to transition well or already have transitioned well. Your next step is doing community well. Without building strong communities many of the talents and skills we have are put on the shelf. Our communities are counting on us to bring those talents to the table. Throughout our military journey, we have learned to do two things extremely well. Lead and Support leaders. Find the Leaders who would benefit from your support. Connect with Leaders in areas that you are passionate about and dive in supporting these Leaders within your communities. I also challenge you to showcase the values-based leadership that has made America's military a world-changing force that accomplishes the mission every time.

Values based leadership is the linchpin in who we are as Veterans. By utilizing our values-based leadership at the local level, we can showcase how we all benefited from the unique alignment of diverse backgrounds that exist within the military. For America to achieve its next Golden Age, we will all have to come together, transition well, and redeploy to our communities. I believe wholeheartedly that the greatest within any community are the ones who fully commit to serving others. I challenge you to commit to service in whatever capacity fits your new lifestyle. Whether that service is at a VSO (Veterans Service Organization) or a Big Brother Big Sister Program your continued commitment to service will take you to places that you never dreamed of or imagined.

One of my mentors shared this with me; Information applied changes situations. I hope some of the information that you gleaned from this book empowers you to make lasting changes in your life. My intention is that once you have transitioned well that you would empower other veterans to do the same. As we commit to serving one another, we will strengthen our communities, our companies, and most importantly our families. You have it in you to continue to make a global impact simply by committing to living life well. You have been trained to seize each day and live life without limits. My challenge to you is why live with limits now.

Notes

Notes

Resource Guide

No one can tell you exactly how to transition, but what they can share is exactly what they did as they transitioned. I hope this Resource Guide connects you with individuals and organizations that enhance your transitions journey.

Organization	Services Provided	Contact Information	Veterans Organizations Type
NoSurrenderInc	Counseling/Mentorship	https://www.nosurrenderinc.com/	Non Profits
Rally Point Six	Training/Career Development	http://rp6.org/	Non Profits
Soldiers' Angels	Disaster Aid, Disaster Preparedness & Relief Services, Human Services, Military & Veterans Organizations, Travelers Aid, Veterans	http://soldiersangels.org/	Non Profits
Veteran Tickets Foundation	Military & Veterans Organizations, Veterans	http://www.vettix.org/	Non Profits
Wounded Warrior Project	Emergency Assistance, Human Services, Military & Veterans Organizations, Veterans	https://www.woundedwarriorproject.org/	Non Profits
Mission in Citrus Inc	Civil Rights, Homeless & Housing, Homeless Shelters, International, Military & Veterans Organizations, Veterans	https://www.missionincitrus.com/	Non Profits
Foundation For American Veterans	Military & Veterans Organizations, Veterans	www.fav.org	Non Profits
Freedom Alliance	Educational and charitable organization	https://freedomalliance.org/	Non Profits
Dogs on Deployment	Animal Protection & Welfare, Animals, Military & Veterans Organizations, Veterans	https://www.dogsondeployment.org/	Non Profits
K9s For Warriors	Animal-Related, Animals, Military & Veterans Organizations, Veterans	https://www.k9sforwarriors.org/	Non Profits

Operation Second Chance Inc	Military & Veterans Organizations, Veterans	http://www.operationsecondchance.org/	Non Profits
Move America Forward	International, Military & Veterans Organizations, National Security, Veterans	http://www.moveamericaforward.org/	Non Profits
Paralyzed Veterans of America	Health, Military & Veterans Organizations, Mutual & Membership Benefit, Nerve, Muscle & Bone Diseases Research, Veterans	http://www.pva.org/site/c.ajIRK9NJLcJ2E/b.6305401/k.27D1/Paralyzed_Veterans_of_America.htm	Non Profits
USA Cares Inc	Emergency Assistance, Homeless & Housing, Housing Expense Reduction Support, Human Services, Military & Veterans Organizations, Veterans	http://www.usacares.org/	Non Profits
Starfish Foundation Inc	Arts & Culture, Arts, Culture & Humanities, Counseling, Mental Health, Military & Veterans Organizations, Veterans	http://www.asterias-starfish.org/en/	Non Profits
Any Soldier Inc.	Human Service Organizations, Human Services, Military & Veterans Organizations, Veterans	http://www.anysoldier.com/index.cfm	Non Profits
Operation Support our Troops America	Military & Veterans Organizations, Veterans	http://www.osotamerica.org/	Non Profits
Tragedy Assistance Program For Survivors	Counseling, Mental Health, Military & Veterans Organizations, Veterans	http://www.taps.org/	Non Profits
Travis Manion Foundation	Human Service Organizations, Human Services, Military & Veterans Organizations, Philanthropy, Public Foundations, Veterans	http://www.travismanion.org/	Non Profits

Coalition To Salute Americas Heroes	Mental Health, Military & Veterans Organizations, Substance Abuse Prevention, Veterans	https://saluteheroes.org/	Non Profits
1Boy4Change, Inc.	Animal-Related, Animals, Health, Health Care, Military & Veterans Organizations, Veterans	http://www.1boy4change.org/	Non Profits
Green Beret Foundation	Civil Rights, Military & Veterans Organizations, Unknown, Veterans	http://www.greenberetfoundation.org/	Non Profits
The Coming Home Project	Military & Veterans Organizations, Veterans	http://www.cominghomeproject.net/	Non Profits
Snowball Express	Human Services, Military & Veterans Organizations, Veterans	https://snowballexpress.org/	Non Profits
H.E.R.O.E.S. Care, Inc.	Emergency Assistance, Human Services, Military & Veterans Organizations, Veterans	https://heroescare.org/	Non Profits
GloverLuck, L.L.P.	Survivor Benefits,Dependent Benefits Pension,Disability Resulting from VA Treatment,Disability Compensation for Physical and Mental Disabilities,Disability Compensation for Physical Disabilities,Disability Compensation for Mental Disabilities,Request for Revision (CUE),Effective Date	http://gloverluck.com/	Advocacy
Asknod Inc.	Disability Compensation for Physical Disabilities,Request for Revision (CUE),Vocational Rehabilitation,Effective Date	http://www.asknod.org	Advocacy

Gumps Victor Alpha Compensation Services, LLC	Survivor Benefits,Dependent Benefits Pension,Disability Resulting from VA Treatment,Disability Compensation for Physical and Mental Disabilities,Request for Revision (CUE),Effective Date	https://www.gumpslegal.com	Advocacy
Fochler Veterans Law	Survivor Benefits,Dependent Benefits Pension,Disability Resulting from VA Treatment,Disability Compensation for Physical and Mental Disabilities,Disability Compensation for Physical Disabilities,Disability Compensation for Mental Disabilities,Request for Revision (CUE),Effective Date	https://www.fochlerveteranslaw.com	Advocacy
Bosley & Bratch	VA Foreclosures,VA Loans,VA Insurance,Survivor Benefits,Dependent Benefits Pension,Disability Compensation for Physical and Mental Disabilities,Request for Revision (CUE),Education Benefits,Effective Date	http://www.lawyers4veterans.com/contact-us/	Advocacy
Attorney at Law	Survivor Benefits,Disability Compensation for Physical and Mental Disabilities,Disability Compensation for Physical Disabilities,Disability Compensation for Mental Disabilities,Effective Date	http://www.cck-law.com	Advocacy

The Law Office of Barry P. Allen	Disability Compensation for Physical and Mental Disabilities,Disability Compensation for Physical Disabilities,Disability Compensation for Mental Disabilities,Request for Revision (CUE),Effective Date	http://www.yourVAadvocate.com	Advocacy
Barry M. Salzman, Attorney at Law	Survivor Benefits,Disability Resulting from VA Treatment,Disability Compensation for Physical and Mental Disabilities,Request for Revision (CUE),Effective Date	http://www.barrysalzman.com	Advocacy
Krause Law, PLLC	Disability Compensation for Physical Disabilities,Disability Compensation for Mental Disabilities,Request for Revision (CUE),Education Benefits,Vocational Rehabilitation,Effective Date,VA Health Benefits,Survivor Benefits,Disability Resulting from VA Treatment,Disability Compensation for Physical and Mental Disabilities	http://www.benjaminkrauselaw.com	Advocacy
Silver & Archibald, LLP	Survivor Benefits,Disability Resulting from VA Treatment,Disability Compensation for Physical and Mental Disabilities,Request for Revision (CUE),Effective Date	http://www.silverandarchibald.com/	Advocacy

Zentz & Zentz	VA Health Benefits,Survivor Benefits,Dependent Benefits Pension,Request for Revision (CUE)	http://zentzlaw.com	Advocacy
Freeman & Freeman	Survivor Benefits,Disability Compensation for Physical and Mental Disabilities,Disability Compensation for Physical Disabilities,Disability Compensation for Mental Disabilities,Request for Revision (CUE),Education Benefits,Vocational Rehabilitation,Effective Date	http://www.freemanlaw	Advocacy
Allsup	Survivor Benefits,Disability Compensation for Physical and Mental Disabilities	https://www.allsup.com	Advocacy
Charles W. Boohar, Jr. Esquire	VA Health Benefits,Survivor Benefits,Dependent Benefits Pension,Apportionment,Disability Resulting from VA Treatment,Disability Compensation for Physical and Mental Disabilities,Disability Compensation for Physical Disabilities,Disability Compensation for Mental Disabilities,Request for Revision (CUE),Effective Date	http://www.compforvets.com	Advocacy

Community Legal Services of Mid-Florida, Inc. (non-profit)	Disability Compensation for Physical and Mental Disabilities,Disability Compensation for Physical Disabilities,Disability Compensation for Mental Disabilities	http://www.clsmf.org/veterans	Advocacy
Shifrin, Newman, Smith, Inc.	Disability Compensation for Physical and Mental Disabilities	http://www.snsdisability.com	Advocacy
Chitwood and Fairbairn, P.A.	Survivor Benefits,Disability Compensation for Physical and Mental Disabilities,Request for Revision (CUE),Effective Date	http://www.wncdisability.com	Advocacy
Manring & Farrell	Disability Compensation for Physical and Mental Disabilities,Request for Revision (CUE),Effective Date	http://www.manringfarrell-socialsecuritylaw.com	Advocacy
Bluestein, Nichols, Thompson, & Delgado, LLC	Survivor Benefits,Disability Resulting from VA Treatment,Disability Compensation for Physical and Mental Disabilities,Disability Compensation for Physical Disabilities,Disability Compensation for Mental Disabilities,Request for Revision (CUE),Effective Date	https://bntdlaw.com	Advocacy
Gardberg & Kemmerly, P.C	Survivor Benefits,Dependent Benefits Pension,Disability Compensation for Physical and Mental Disabilities,Request for Revision (CUE),Effective Date	http://www.gardberglaw.com	Advocacy

Dale Burnell, LLC	Survivor Benefits,Disability Compensation for Physical Disabilities,Disability Compensation for Mental Disabilities,Request for Revision (CUE),Effective Date	http://www.veteranrights.net	Advocacy
Dan Curry	Survivor Benefits,Disability Resulting from VA Treatment,Disability Compensation for Physical and Mental Disabilities,Effective Date	http://www.brownandcurry.com	Advocacy
Tuley Law Office	Survivor Benefits,Disability Resulting from VA Treatment,Disability Compensation for Physical and Mental Disabilities,Disability Compensation for Physical Disabilities,Disability Compensation for Mental Disabilities,Request for Revision (CUE)	http://www.tuleylaw.com	Advocacy
Royle Law Office, PS, Inc.	VA Disability Law, Survivor Benefits, Dependent Benefits Pension, Disability Resulting from VA Treatment, Disability Compensation for Physical and Mental Disabilities, Request for Revision (CUE), Effective Date	http://www.roylelaw.com/	Advocacy

Michigan Veterans Law	VA Health Benefits,Survivor Benefits,Dependent Benefits Pension,Disability Resulting from VA Treatment,Disability Compensation for Physical and Mental Disabilities,Request for Revision (CUE),Effective Date	http://www.mivetlaw.com/	Advocacy
Darrin Class, Attorney at Law	Survivor Benefits,Dependent Benefits Pension,Disability Compensation for Physical and Mental Disabilities,Disability Compensation for Physical Disabilities,Disability Compensation for Mental Disabilities,Request for Revision (CUE)	http://www.rdclasslegal. com	Advocacy
Justice Legal Group	Survivor Benefits,Disability Resulting from VA Treatment,Disability Compensation for Physical and Mental Disabilities,Disability Compensation for Physical Disabilities,Disability Compensation for Mental Disabilities,Request for Revision (CUE),Effective Date	https://www. justicelegalgroup.com	Advocacy

Bonner Di Salvo, PLLC	Survivor Benefits,Dependent Benefits Pension,Apportionment,Disability Resulting from VA Treatment,Disability Compensation for Physical and Mental Disabilities,Disability Compensation for Physical Disabilities,Disability Compensation for Mental Disabilities,Request for Revision (CUE),Education Benefits,Effective Date	http://www.bonnerdisalvo.com	Advocacy
Peterson & Fishman, PLLP	Survivor Benefits,Dependent Benefits Pension,Disability Resulting from VA Treatment,Disability Compensation for Physical and Mental Disabilities,Request for Revision (CUE),Effective Date	http://www. PetersonandFishman.com	Advocacy
Hawaii Disability Legal Services, LLLC	Dependent Benefits Pension,Disability Compensation for Physical and Mental Disabilities,Disability Compensation for Physical Disabilities,Disability Compensation for Mental Disabilities,Request for Revision (CUE),Effective Date	http://www. hawaiidisabilitylegal.com	Advocacy

Bosley & Bratch	Disability Resulting from VA Treatment,Disability Compensation for Physical and Mental Disabilities,Disability Compensation for Physical Disabilities,Disability Compensation for Mental Disabilities,Request for Revision (CUE),Effective Date	http://www.lawyers4veterans.com	Advocacy
Shea, Kohl, Alessi & Kuhl LC	Survivor Benefits,Dependent Benefits Pension,Disability Compensation for Physical and Mental Disabilities,Disability Compensation for Physical Disabilities,Disability Compensation for Mental Disabilities,Request for Revision (CUE),Effective Date	https://www.SKAKLAW.com	Advocacy
Kugal Disability Law Group	Disability Compensation for Physical and Mental Disabilities,Disability Compensation for Physical Disabilities,Disability Compensation for Mental Disabilities,Request for Revision (CUE),Effective Date	http://www.kugaldisabilitylawgroup.com	Advocacy
Disability Attorneys of Michigan	Disability Compensation for Physical and Mental Disabilities	http://damichigan.com/	Advocacy

Goodman, Allen, Donnelly	Survivor Benefits,Dependent Benefits Pension,Disability Resulting from VA Treatment,Disability Compensation for Physical and Mental Disabilities,Disability Compensation for Physical Disabilities,Disability Compensation for Mental Disabilities,Request for Revision (CUE),Effective Date	http://www.goodmanallen.com	Advocacy
Bluestein, Nichols, Thompson & Delgado Law	Survivor Benefits,Dependent Benefits Pension,Disability Resulting from VA Treatment,Disability Compensation for Physical and Mental Disabilities,Disability Compensation for Physical Disabilities,Disability Compensation for Mental Disabilities,Effective Date	http://bntdlaw.com/	Advocacy
Veterans Legal Adovocates, P.A	Survivor Benefits,Apportionment,Disability Resulting from VA Treatment,Disability Compensation for Physical and Mental Disabilities,Disability Compensation for Physical Disabilities,Disability Compensation for Mental Disabilities,Effective Date	http://www.vetslegalhelp.com	Advocacy
The Narvaez Law Office, P.A.	Disability Compensation for Physical and Mental Disabilities	http://www.attorneyfernando.com	Advocacy

MeetMyShoes	Survivor Benefits,Disability Compensation for Physical and Mental Disabilities,Education Benefits	http://www.meetmyshoes.org	Advocacy
Francis White Law PLLC	Request for Revision (CUE),Education Benefits,Vocational Rehabilitation,Effective Date,Survivor Benefits, Apportionment,Disabi lity Resulting from VA Treatment,Disability Compensation for Physical and Mental Disabilities	http://www. franciswhitelaw.com	Advocacy
Deuterman Law Group	Disability Compensation for Physical and Mental Disabilities,Request for Revision (CUE),Effective Date	http://www.Deutermanlaw.com	Advocacy
Piemonte Law Firm	Survivor Benefits,Disability Compensation for Physical and Mental Disabilities,Disability Compensation for Physical Disabilities,Disability Compensation for Mental Disabilities,Request for Revision (CUE),Effective Date	http://www. piemontelawfirm.com	Advocacy
Attorney At Law	VA Health Benefits,Survivor Benefits,Dependent Benefits Pension,Disability Resulting from VA Treatment,Disability Compensation for Physical and Mental Disabilities,Effective Date	http://GinaDinesHolness.com	Advocacy

After Service, LLC	Survivor Benefits,Dependent Benefits Pension,Disability Compensation for Physical and Mental Disabilities,Request for Revision (CUE),Effective Date	http://AfterService.com	Advocacy
Hugh D. Cox, Attorney at Law	Survivor Benefits, Dependent Benefits Pension, Disability Resulting from VA Treatment, Disability Compensation for Physical and Mental Disabilities, Request for Revision (CUE), Effective Date,	http://www.hughcox.com	Advocacy
Perkins Studdard, LLC	Survivor Benefits,Dependent Benefits Pension,Disability Resulting from VA Treatment,Disability Compensation for Physical and Mental Disabilities,Disability Compensation for Physical Disabilities,Disability Compensation for Mental Disabilities,Request for Revision (CUE),Effective Date	http://www. winyourvetclaim.com	Advocacy
Connor Law	Survivor Benefits,Dependent Benefits Pension,Disability Resulting from VA Treatment,Disability Compensation for Physical and Mental Disabilities,Request for Revision (CUE),Effective Date	http://www.jeconnor.com	Advocacy

Elie Halpern & Associates, PLLC	Disability Compensation for Physical and Mental Disabilities,Disability Compensation for Physical Disabilities,Disability Compensation for Mental Disabilities,Request for Revision (CUE),Effective Date	http://www.ssavalaw.com	Advocacy
N.M.L.B. Veterans Advocacy Group, Inc.	VA Health Benefits,Survivor Benefits,Disability Resulting from VA Treatment,Disability Compensation for Physical and Mental Disabilities,Disability Compensation for Physical Disabilities,Disability Compensation for Mental Disabilities,Request for Revision (CUE),Education Benefits,Effective Date	http://www.nmlbvet.com	Advocacy
Perkins Studdard, LLC	Survivor Benefits,Dependent Benefits Pension,Disability Compensation for Physical and Mental Disabilities,Effective Date	http://www.winyourvetclaim.com	Advocacy
Black & Davison	VA Health Benefits,Survivor Benefits,Disability Compensation for Physical and Mental Disabilities,Disability Compensation for Physical Disabilities,Disability Compensation for Mental Disabilities,Request for Revision (CUE),Effective Date	http://www.blackanddavison.com	Advocacy

The Law Office of John M. Williams, LLC	Disability Compensation for Physical and Mental Disabilities,Disability Compensation for Physical Disabilities,Disability Compensation for Mental Disabilities,Request for Revision (CUE),Effective Date	http://jmwilliamslaw.com	Advocacy
Bergmann & Moore	We are dedicated to serving the needs of Veterans in compensation claims before and against the Department of Veterans Affairs. Managed by former Department of Veterans Affairs Attorneys, we have a proven track record of providing unparalleled legal representation to disabled Veterans and their dependents.	http://www.vetlawyers.com/	Advocacy
Transition Assistance Program		http://www.benefits.va.gov/tap/	Transition Programs
Iraq and Afghanistan Veterans of America (IAVA)	Iraq and Afghanistan Veterans of America (IAVA) is a nonprofit, nonpartisan organization representing new veterans and their families. IAVA is dedicated to standing with the veterans of Iraq and Afghanistan.	http://iava.org/	Transition Programs
National Association of American Veterans (NAAV)	"Veteran Employment And Training Opportunities"	http://www.naavets.org/	Transition Programs
American Legion	Wartime veterans service organization aimed at advocating patriotism across the U.S. through diverse programs and...	https://www.legion.org/	Transition Programs

Wounded Warrior Project	Emergency Assistance, Human Services, Military & Veterans Organizations, Veterans	https://www.woundedwarriorproject.org/	Transition Programs
Veterans of Foreign Wars (VFW)		http://www.vfw.org/	Transition Programs
AMVETS		http://www.amvets.org/	Transition Programs
America Wants You		https://www.facebook.com/AmericaWantsYou/	Transition Programs
Veterans Support Organization (VSO)		https://www.va.gov/vso/	Transition Programs
USO	"The USO strengthens America's military service members by keeping them connected to family, home and country, throughout their service to the nation."	https://www.uso.org/	Transition Programs
VetJobs	"VetJobs services makes it easy to reach transitioning military, National Guard, Reserve Component Members and veterans that have separated over the last several decades and, due to the services provided by VetJobs, are now productive members of the civilian work force in all disciplines as well as their family members."	http://vetjobs.com/	Transition Programs
Military Exits	"This is a great site for those in transition from military to civilian life."	http://www.militaryexits.com/	Transition Programs
US Department of Veterans Affairs Veteran Entrepreneur Portal	Business Development Portal	https://www.va.gov/osdbu/entrepreneur/	Entrepreneurship

Helmets To Hardhats (H2H)	"H2H connects military service members to building and apprenticeship programs. Veterans learn a trade at state-of-the-art training facilities. "	http://www. helmetstohardhats.org/	Entrepreneurship
Brooklyn Navy Yard Employment Center	The Employment Center was established in 1999 and has placed approximately 1,600 jobs. The Center identifies, screens and places veterans seeking work in local jobs such as entry-level industrial, warehouse and customer service positions.	http://bldg92.org/	Entrepreneurship
Brooklyn Workforce Innovations:	B.W.I. operates four job training programs that prepares veterans for careers in commercial driving, cabling, carpentry and television/film production. The programs also leverage strong relationships with local employers to target salaried jobs with generous benefits packages.	http://www.bwiny.org/	Entrepreneurship

Workforce1 Veterans Services :	"Veterans Employment Specialists at Workforce1 Career Centers across the City offer intensive career services and job placement opportunities to veterans and their spouses. They work with employers committed to hiring veterans. As a result, Workforce1 is connecting more veterans to stable and meaningful employment. Veteran Specialist are located at the following Workforce1 Career Centers. Appointments are encouraged."	http://www.nyc.gov/html/sbs/wf1/html/about/veterans.shtml	Entrepreneurship
Navoba	NAVOBA OPENS DOORS FOR VETERAN-OWNED BUSINESSES	http://www.navoba.com/	Entrepreneurship
Veteranscorp.org	The Veteranscorp. org mission is to help structure and facilitate collaborations between nonprofit and profit small business entities and veteran/service disabled veteran owned small businesses.	http://www.veteranscorp.org/	Entrepreneurship

SBA Veterans Advantage Loan Program	The Small Business Administration's Veteran Advantage Loan Program, housed under the Express Loan program, expedites applications for government-backed loans of up to $350,000. You are guaranteed a response to your application within 36 hours. Normally, there is a fee of 3 % of the guaranteed amount of the loan. But now through September, if you are approved, the SBA will waive all upfront guarantee fees for vets. (These fees are waived for all applicants, not just vets, through the end of the fiscal year for loans under $150K). Typically you'll need a credit score above 680 to qualify for an SBA loan. Check your score here for free.	http://www.sba.gov/news	Entrepreneurship
Women Veterans Igniting the Spirit of Entrepreneurship (V-WISE)	V-Wise is an SBA-sponsored training program for women veterans. The 3-day conference provides advice on starting a business as well as growing an existing business. It's a great networking opportunity as it attracts other business owners or business owners-to-be from around the country. Hotel accommodation, all meals except one, and books/program materials are entirely covered. You are responsible for travel to and from the conference.	http://whitman.syr.edu/VWise/faqs.aspx	Entrepreneurship

Entrepreneurship Bootcamp for Veterans with Disabilities (EBV)	The Institute for Veterans and Military Families at Syracuse University started the EBV program with the goal of creating entrepreneurs by the end of the 3 phase program. Phase 1 is a 30-day instructor led online course covering the basics of owning and running a business. Phase 2 is a 9-day residency at a host university where students tackle business issues hands on. Finally, Phase 3 involves 12 months of ongoing support from EBV mentors, a great resource if you have questions (and you're likely to!) after setting up your business. Travel expenses, lodging, meals, program materials, textbooks, and all other costs are covered by the program.	http://ebv.vets.syr.edu/veterans/	Entrepreneurship
The Bunker – Startup Incubator	The Bunker is an incubator for veteran-owned technology startups. For six months, The Bunker will provide you with office space where you can work on your business, talk to a network of fellow entrepreneurs, obtain mentorship and professional development, and access capital from investors. There are roundtable conversations, networking events, and a speaker series designed for the businesses in the program.	https://bunkerlabs.org/about-the-bunker/	Entrepreneurship

SCORE Veteran Fast Launch Initiative – Free Software and Templates	The SCORE Foundation has a network of over 13,000 mentors, trainers, and partners. Through this network, as part of their Veteran Fast Launch Initiative, SCORE provides numerous resources. This includes free business workshops; one-on-one mentoring; free business calculators, templates, and spreadsheets; and 5 free hours of financial advice from a Certified Public Accountant. There are 320 chapters, so you can go into a local SCORE office today for more info.	https://www.score.org/content/veteran-fast-launch-initiative	Entrepreneurship
Hivers and Strivers — Investment in Veteran-Owned Businesses	Hivers and Strivers, an angel investment firm, focuses on early stage investments to support startup companies founded and run by graduates of the U.S. Military Academies (West Point, Coast Guard, Annapolis, and Air Force). The firm invests anywhere from $250,000 to $1 million in a single round. If you're seeking more than $1 million, you can use the Hivers and Strivers network to find other investors. Veterans can complete an online application.	http://www.hiversandstrivers.com/	Entrepreneurship

| Vocational Rehabilitation & Employment Program for Disabled Vets | The U.S. Department of Veterans Affairs runs a Vocational Rehabilitation & Employment (V&RE) Program for veterans that have become disabled as a result of their service. The seriousness of the service-connected disability determines the amount of funding you can receive. Veterans can receive grants for the purchase of inventory, supplies, licensing fees, and essential equipment. Applicants must submit a complete business plan before they can be considered for funding. We recommend using LivePlan business plan software to make drawing up a business plan easier. They have many templates and examples to choose from plus they have a 60-day money back guarantee. | http://www.benefits.va.gov/vocrehab/ | Entrepreneurship |
| Veterans' Opportunity Fund – Venture Capital | The Veterans' Opportunity Fund, run by TCP Venture Capital, invests up to $3 million in high-growth veteran-owned businesses. They focus on east coast businesses involved in technology, healthcare, and business services. To be considered, you should have some early revenue or a prototype product or service that can be evaluated. | http://tcp.vc/funds/veterans-opportunity-fund/ | Entrepreneurship |

St. Michael's Veterans Campus	"St. Michael's Veterans Center is uniquely designed to offer safe, permanent housing combined with wraparound support services to enable and empower a successful transition to productive and healthy civilian living. They also provide services for mental health and substance abuse counseling, peer-to-peer mentoring, employment readiness and job skills training, transportation, legal support, referrals for education or GED instruction, and assistance in obtaining local, state and/or federal benefits."	https://www.catholiccharities-kcsj.org/portfolio-view/veterans-services/	Social Services
Veterans Come Home Program	The services of the "Veterans Come Home Program" day program are: homeless prevention, meals, showers, clothing, counseling, leadership and job training, transportation, financial aid, educational classes, and a drop-in day center.	http://keepourveteranssafe.com/vets_come_home_program.htm	Social Services
Work of Honor	Career Site	https://www.workofhonor.com/	Career
The Walt Disney Company	Veteran Hiring	http://heroesworkhere.disney.com/	Career
CACI	Veteran Hiring	http://careers.caci.com/page/show/veterans	Career
Ryder	Veteran Hiring	https://ryder.com/careers/military-recruitment	Career
Army & Air Force Exchange Service	Veteran Hiring	https://odin.aafes.com/employment/EXCHANGE_EMPLOYMENT/HTML/start.html	Career

Stack-UpOrg
@StackUpDotOrg
https://twitter.com/StackUpDotOrg

Student Veterans
@studentvets
https://twitter.com/studentvets

Veterans in Tech
@VeteransInTech
https://twitter.com/VeteransInTech

Jake Wood
@JakeWoodTR
https://twitter.com/JakeWoodTR

Justin Brown
@1justinbrown
https://twitter.com/1justinbrown

Elizabeth McCormick
@pilotspeaker
https://twitter.com/pilotspeaker

Got Your 6
@GotYourSix
https://twitter.com/GotYourSix

Frank X. Shaw
@fxshaw
https://twitter.com/fxshaw

5. International Traffic in Arms Regulation (ITAR) ISBN: 97809816288

ARMY TOPICS

1. Ranger Handbook SH 21-76 ISBN-13: 978-1936800087

2. US Army Physical Readiness Training TC 3.22-20 ISBN:97809816240

3. US Army Physical Fitness Training FM 21-20 ISBN:97809816240

4. US Army Leadership FM 6-22 ISBN: 978-0981620671

5. US Army Drill and Ceremonies FM 3-21.5 ISBN: 978-1936800025

Baxter International	Veteran Hiring	http://www.baxter.com/careers/working-at-baxter/jobs-for-military-veterans.page	Career
Sprint	Veteran Hiring	https://www.sprint.jobs/content/military/	Career
Booz Allen Hamilton	Veteran Hiring	http://www.boozallen.com/insights/better-our-world/supporting-veterans	Career
Comcast NBCUniversal	Veteran Hiring	http://jobs.comcast.com/military	Career
Ernst & Young LLP	Veteran Hiring	http://www.ey.com/us/en/about-us/our-values/ey-is-dedicated-to-supporting-veterans---0---overview	Career
Price Waterhouse Coopers	Veteran Hiring	http://www.pwc.com/us/en/careers/experienced/why-pwc/military-veterans.html	Career
Hormel Foods	Veteran Hiring	http://www.hormelfoods.com/Careers/MilitaryRecruitment/Military-Recruitment	Career
Deloitte	Veteran Hiring	http://military-veteran-jobs.deloitte.com/	Career
KPMG LLP	Veteran Hiring	http://kpmg-veterans.jobs/	Career
PNC Bank	Veteran Hiring	https://www.pnc.com/en/about-pnc/topics/pnc-pov/commentary/pnc-pov-damien-gottschalk-hiring-veterans.html	Career
JPMorgan Chase	Veteran Hiring	https://www.jpmorganchase.com/corporate/Corporate-Responsibility/military-veterans.htm	Career
Kelly Services	Veteran Hiring	http://www.kellyservices.us/US/Business-Services/Hire-Veterans/	Career
WilsonHCG	Veteran Hiring	http://www.wilsonhcg.com/veteran-recruitment	Career
Prudential Financial	Veteran Hiring	http://corporate.prudential.com/view/page/corp/31840	Career
The Principal Financial Group	Veteran Hiring	https://www.principal.com/about-us/careers	Career

Humana	Veteran Hiring	http://www.jobs.net/jobs/humana-veterans/en-us/	Career
Accenture	Veteran Hiring	https://www.accenture.com/us-en/careers/find-your-fit-military-cleared-professionals	Career
Northrop Grumman	Veteran Hiring	http://www.northropgrumman.com/careers/MilitaryVeterans/Pages/default.aspx	Career
USAA	Veteran Hiring	https://www.usaajobs.com/military/	Career
VA Vocational Rehabilitation and Employment Home	"You may receive vocational rehabilitation and employment services to help with job training, employment accommodations, resume development, and job seeking skills coaching. Other services may be provided to assist Veterans in starting their own businesses or independent living services for those who are severely disabled and unable to work in traditional employment."	http://www.benefits.va.gov/vocrehab/	Career
VA Employment Programs for Homeless Veterans	"VA's Compensated Work Therapy (CWT) is a national vocational program comprised of three unique programs which assist homeless Veterans in returning to competitive employment: Sheltered Workshop, Transitional Work, and Supported Employment. Veterans in CWT are paid at least the federal or state minimum wage, whichever is higher."	http://www.va.gov/homeless/employment_programs.asp	Career

American Job Centers	"America's Service Locator connects individuals to employment and training opportunities available at local American Job Centers. The website provides contact information for a range of local work-related services, including unemployment benefits, career development, and educational opportunities."	http://www.servicelocator.org/	Career
Department of Labor, Women Vets Site	The Women Veterans site at the U.S. Department of Labor	http://www.dol.gov/vets/womenveterans/	Career
Dress for Succes	The mission of Dress for Success is to promote the economic independence of disadvantaged women by providing professional attire, and a network of support and career development tools to help women thrive in work and in life.	http://www.dressforsuccess.org/	Career
National Veterans Foundation Job Board	A listing of jobs across the country at companies interested in hiring veterans.	http://nvf.org/jobs	Career
Work for Warriors (Guard and Reserve)	"Job Postings & Unit Vacancies. The California Military Department is a diverse, community-based organization comprised of four pillars: the California Army National Guard, the California Air National Guard, the California State Military Reserve and the California Youth and Community Programs."	http://www.calguard.ca.gov/jobs	Career

Small Business (SBA Veteran & Disabled Veterans)	If you are a veteran or service-disabled veteran, SBA has resources to help you start and grow your small business.	http://www.calguard.ca.gov/jobs	Career
GE	Veteran Hiring	https://www.ge.com/careers/culture/us-veterans	Career
Cigna	Veteran Hiring	https://www.cigna.com/careers/united-states/veterans	Career

About The Author

In Veteran's Transition: A Contact Sport, Bernard Bergan
presents a winning manual you'll want to keep with you as
you prepare to transition well. It is a terrific resource for anyone seeking to self-assess on their transitions journey and
dedicate themselves to finding purpose after military service.
Using this tool, each of us can bring immediate value to the
Veteran's transition process at the individual, organizational,
and corporate level.

Bernard Bergan spent six years serving within the Special
Operations Community. He then successfully navigated a
first of its kind technology training program to Corporate IT.
He now resides in Seattle Washington with his family where
he continues his work and Veterans Advocacy.

Veteran Thought
Leaders to Follow on Twitter

Jasism
@JasBoothe1
https://twitter.com/JasBoothe1

Vets2PM
@Vets2PM
https://twitter.com/Vets2PM

Ryen Macababbad
@Ryen_Mac
https://twitter.com/Ryen_Mac

Vet Advocate, Renée
@ReneeH4MVA2016
https://twitter.com/ReneeH4MVA2016

Patrick J. MurphyVerified account
@USAMurphy
https://twitter.com/USAMurphy

Glenn Banton, Sr.
@glennbanton
https://twitter.com/glennbanton

Anthony Seo
@anthony_seo
https://twitter.com/anthony_seo

Tegan Griffith
@teg8403
https://twitter.com/teg8403

WIMSA
@wimsatweets
https://twitter.com/wimsatweets

Paul (PJ) Rieckhoff
@PaulRieckhoff
https://twitter.com/PaulRieckhoff

Military-Transition
@miltransurvey
https://twitter.com/miltransurvey

Jocko Willink
@jockowillink
https://twitter.com/jockowillink

Jeremy Pitman
@pitmanjd
https://twitter.com/pitmanjd

OSDVerified account
@OpSupplyDrop
https://twitter.com/OpSupplyDrop

Stephen Machuga
@ShanghaiSix
https://twitter.com/ShanghaiSix